Listen to the Wind
Speak from the Heart
Copyright 2010 by Wakiya Records and Roger Gilbert. All
rights reserved.
Printed in the United States of America. No part of this
book may be used or reproduced in any manor whatsoever
without written permission.
ISBN 1450572529 EAN-13 9781450572521

Design and art by Roger Thunderhands Gilbert

"Dedicated to my Son Aaron and my Grandson Miles."

Introduction

Knowing Thunderhands has been akin to knowing the
difference between wisdom and passion, and how both can
be indivisible in the essence of one man. Same question.
same answer. Thunder is a master healer. He asks that you
not follow him, just hear him, and listen, see him, and
attend. Why? Because your a free spirit and can do
whatever you want. But I suggest that you do come in for
awhile and partake in Thunder's banquet fit for a Taoist
feast! What is Tao? Tao isn't an abstraction, it's Tao, it is
Earth and universal spirituality.

A doctor saved my body, an educator saved my intellect, an
employer saved my livelihood, and a spiritual healer saved
my soul, in that order. I was facing death and could not
reach deep enough into spirituality to save myself. The
doctor revived and restored me. Now, I am free to travel
with Thunder, a spiritual healer, my friend, and a Gift of
Grace. My gratitude to him is like a clear, river ever-
evolving to become an ocean, a galaxy, a universe, and
more.
 Ilene "Arrow" Sandman, MA
Professor of Humanities

Preface

There isn't much I want to write concerning this book because I don't want the reader to have any pre-conceived notions. I would rather you read it and take from it what serves you. Needless to say I don't consider this a self help book, but more of a "Spirit Help" book of counsel, or thoughts for consideration.

The title is self explanatory in a way. However the term "Listening to the Wind" is from the Native American tradition, as is speaking from the heart, or the one eye of the heart (Chante Ista). My view of listening to the wind is listening to what nature, the universe, and your higher self is telling you, or maybe telling you to pass on to others. Speaking from the heart is conveying the messages you get from listening to the wind. It can also mean speaking straight and not with a forked tongue.

You travel the road of life and you write about things, and maybe these things will strike a chord with others. I leave it to Great Spirit as to whether or not this is meaningful for you. My intention is that some kind of healing will take place from the thoughts that I am offering for consideration. I believe in the old ways where a counsel of elders would sit around a campfire and speak their thoughts. Take it in that spirit. So no table of contents, open the book to any page or read in any order.

Mitakuye Oyasin
(all my relations)
Thunderhands

Internal Strength

It's all about internal strength, honor and true humility, not if you win or lose, live or die etc. It's how you live your life, I.E. not worrying about it. Not considering so much about right and wrongs on the outside, or what someone else is doing that may be right or wrong. Strengthen the inner, refuse to do battle with the opponents within and without so to speak. Refuse to confront the oncoming thrust of the sword, better to step aside and watch it miss it's mark. Or better yet take no thought on it. Hold no malice or anger for anything. Keep working on that inner light or the superior self, because that serves the better good. Work towards peace and harmony within and it will be reflected without. Sometimes you can win a battle, but that doesn't mean you win the war. Peace and harmony within brings good fortune for all concerned. It's about motive, we bring sorrow on ourselves and others by not being true to our higher self or good. It's like practicing the martial arts for glory and ego, or practicing it to strengthen mind, body, and spirit, and to build character and humility. Its not about winning even though you know you can. No matter what might face us, whether it be loneliness, relationships, or any kind of hardship. If we have that internal strength and we walk with the sage, everything will be OK, as within so without. These words are easier to say, then put into practice. And I guess that should be our goal, maybe we can't be perfect but we can work towards an ideal. Sometimes it does take a change in attitude or events that causes a turning point in our lives.

Being A Spiritual Warrior

Being a spiritual warrior is fighting battles that try to entrap you in the emotional games of this so-called reality. Most adults have scars and wounds on their souls after being in the matrix of Maya, or the illusion of this world. The spiritual reality of this battle is about healing and protecting. Healing what others have inflicted upon you, and what you perceive that you have done to others. And by warding off dark energy that comes in different forms in this seemingly never ending drama called the third dimension.

Spiritual warriors study the martial arts and meditation techniques to prepare them to wield the sword of the spirit. They walk with one foot in the spirit world, and one foot in the illusory reality. They take back and strengthen their personal power until it is strong, stable, and in balance. The fire of their spirit is strong, so they can balance others that they meet, while warding off their negativity and dark energy. It is about not believing everything you hear or have been indoctrinated with, since most of it was to serve others purposes and most times consisted of lies or half truths at best. Some people think what they have been indoctrinated with is good for you to, and so they brainwash you from birth. Spiritual warriors find their own way by returning to the real truth or the source. This source will empower them to do battle, in a unique way, using spiritual weaponry.

It's all about energy, and duality. The spiritual warrior within you removes that which is blocking your way and the obstacles in your path. This can include anything such as addiction, attachment to the lower physical realm, and dis-ease of body, mind, and spirit. This can be outside yourself in the form of people who need to be cured, and others that need to be eliminated from your life. If they have a fossilized mentality and belief system filled with hate, let spirit guide you to release them from your presence and to protect the ones you know could be affected by this entity. The spiritual warrior has a type of vision that sees beyond the apparent form or illusion and cuts through the veil. The spiritual warrior has learned control and how to energy shift and deal with any situation. The spiritual warrior is a soldier of the cosmos and universal mind which directs them to do battle by healing, and peaceful methods while still having the power of a warrior. Being a spiritual warrior is learning the sword of no sword, and "Mushin" which are the techniques of emptying the mind so spirit can work through them. It is the highest calling, because a warrior is a healer in the greatest sense of the word. It's a fine line that they walk and requires seeing with the third eye and feeling with extra senses. With warrior-ship comes the blessings of the spirit and the curse or responsibility of knowing and feeling things many have no clue of. This includes, empathy and feelings you pick up on and have to deal with while keeping yourself protected and centered. Does this calling sound hard? It becomes easier the more you let your self be directed from above. As above so below. Everyone has the potential to train and be a spiritual warrior, do you hear the calling? I hope so we need you. If your not part of the solution your become part of the problem.

Walking the Sacred circle

Some times we think as "human beings" that we need to go to others for something that Mother Earth and Grandfather Sky have an abundance of. We may think we want a companion and help mate to give us love, support and validation. That is OK and is a good thing. But do we try to hook up with people that are not walking our path just to have somebody, anybody? I suggest that the marvels of Mother Earth and her energy can supply me with an abundance of love, joy, and nurturing until the "Earth Woman" I want shows up. Where is there more feminine energy then in Unci, Maka, Grandmother Earth? And where can you get more elder energy, or strong counsel then from "Tunkashila" Grandfather Sky? Take a walk in the trees, lose yourself, and connect with the spirit that moves in all things. The trees, rocks, grass, and earth heal you with their auras. All of the plants, animals, and rocks (Inyan) have their own energy field, are you aware of that? Do you feel it? Do you let it mix with your aura? Do you let the wind blow the darkness from your soul? Do you listen to, and ride on the wind, like brother Hawk, Crow, and Eagle? These are not just words Mita Cola! The animals do a dance for you. In the sky it's the winged one's, on the ground it is the critters, the four leggeds. They will never lie to you, judge you, or send you dark energy. They will heal you with their antics and make you smile. The garden path they lead you down is the real one, it's the Red Road. They will never double cross you, or think that you are crazy! Their friendship is a given and only requires our acceptance. Don't turn your back on it, because life here is to short. Yes there are people around us to, and they need to be healed, and I love the two leggeds also. But when you give your love, it is like trusting that they won't use what is given to them to hurt you. Protection is needed when healing and loving. Not all appreciate the wise counsel and love given. You will know by their actions, deeds and words. You will also know by their dealings, and the people they surround themselves with. Are they centered and balanced. Its about love not confusion. The critters are centered and balanced all the time, because they walk in "the sacred circle."

Animal Totems

Do you know your animal totem? If you want to enhance your relationship with great spirit or the spirit that moves in all things, it might be a good idea to identify your totem. The further we get away from nature and our past connection with our shamanistic origins, the less we feel our connection. This is a sad loss for many reasons. Our totem can give us the power we need to overcome obstacles presented to us in this journey we call life. Anyone who owns a domestic animal will testify to the healing properties and love that they can impart to us. What animals do you identify with, dream about, or see on a regular basis? This could well be your totem. Each animal has a gift for you, so it would be beneficial to study the habits, and spiritual properties of your totem or any animal or beast in the natural realm.

Spirit will appear, talk to and guide you on your path through various animals. Go to the park, forest or natural area and make note of the four leggeds or winged ones that come into your view. Even a lizard on a rock is speaking to you. You can talk to them in a soft kind voice and they will respond with a healing or direction for you to take. Meditate and ask that your totem come to you. Ask great spirit to reveal them to you. You can have more then one totem. One of the sky and one of the earth, or more then one of each. One to help you in any circumstance in life. I was once doing a meditation, and my feet got cold. Much to my amazement a bear appeared and lay in a fetal position around my feet sending warm energy and love through my whole body.

I immediately realized that this was a totem animal that had been present in my life before, and as I opened my eyes I glanced at the Zuni bear fetish on my shelf that I had not been paying attention to. That night I put it next to my bed and thanked great spirit for reawakening my relationship with this powerful and yet loving animal. .

The Taoist Warrior

The Taoist warrior, speaks only to guide. The Taoist warrior, prefers silence because his guidance often falls on deaf ears, and so he leads by example. The Taoist warrior realizes "the sword of no sword." The Taoist warrior cares not for the mundane and trivial of which most of the world is comprised, excepting nature.

The Taoist warrior realizes that concepts of right and wrong are just that, concepts. The Taoist warrior cuts to the core without touching the bone. The Taoist warrior is not so concerned with morality, and right or wrong, because one mans right is another man's wrong, and one mans morality is another mans immorality.

The Taoist warrior realizes the past and future are a foggy mist that can't be grasped. The Taoist warrior realizes all wars and enemies are generated from within. The Taoist warrior answers to no one, but walks with the Tao, which doesn't require answers, judge, or assign blame. The Taoist Warrior realizes guilt, fear, and anger are a figment of the mind generated by earthly concepts and conditioning.

The Taoist warrior prefers nature and living alone. The Taoist warrior, is a spiritual warrior and a spiritual man. The Taoist warrior is perfect in that he is not perfect according to the ways of the world. The Taoist warrior is a traveler and wanderer, within and without. The Taoist warrior is often mistaken for having a cold heart, because he realizes detachment is true compassion, for self and others.

The Taoist warrior is a calling few can comprehend, for

how can the Tao be comprehended. The Taoist warrior doesn't comprehend, the Taoist warrior just is. The Taoist warrior realizes that he doesn't know, and that not knowing is the way of realization. The Taoist warrior, can seem like a contradiction to others, for all things change and he flows with the change. This is called walking with the Tao!

Violence on our senses

The culture we live in, the governments, and the social structure as a whole are committing violence against our senses. It is perpetuated by greed. We live in a reality that has departed from right thinking and that is out balance.

Our sense of hearing is bombarded daily by alarming sounds. Loud machine noises abound everywhere in the sky and on earth. The sirens wail, the din of the freeway noise is continuous, and the media blares on and on about the sensational graphic situations on the planet. Loud boom boxes in cars cruise by while garbage dumpsters are smashed violently against the ground. It is hard to hear the birds singing, the water in the streams flowing, and the wind blowing through the trees. It is hard to hear the summer rains and thunder.

Our sense of smell is accosted by the noxious fumes and pollution produced by gas burning vehicles, power plants, and industry. It is difficult to stop and smell the roses or lilac and newly mown fields. Our sense of touch and feeling is being restricted by the concrete and asphalt poured over mother earth, so that we cannot feel the grass between our toes, and walk barefooted as nature intended. The heat rises from the concrete structures causing a rise in temperature and preventing the breeze from blowing on our skin.

Our sense of taste is being dulled by processed foods and that quick snack at the local fast food joint. Food doesn't taste like it used to. Our sense of sight is sickened at the rape of mother earth. Trees are hacked down, and bushes are trimmed to cubicle forms to fit in with the square mentality and the box like structures we live in. No more circles and circle of life. Parks are turned into parking lots. Animals are shot and taken down because of their confusion on the intrusion.

And finally our sense of responsibility, fairness and freedom are being dulled, by the patriarchal system of greed, false power and pride. The current mentality is grab all you can while you can. The nature of man is no nature at all.

So as a result we begin to shut down our senses. We narrow our view so as not to see. We dim our senses of smelling, feeling, and tasting because we don't like what we are being subjected to. We long for nature, and times past from our ancestral memory. We pray for a place of silence in nature where we can gather our thoughts and return to some kind of normalcy. We ache to get off the treadmill of forced labor and slavery just to exist, and get back to oneness with mother earth as hunters and gatherers.

What can we do, what is the way out? Start by taking responsibility for your actions. Think coherently. Its hard, because of the dulling of our sense of fairness to ourselves and others. Don't accept the status quot, and gently nudge yourself into another way of living. Start by turning off the TV and media brainwashing machine. If you can't find nature, start by having a small Zen fountain in your home with the running water. Or buy a CD with the sounds of running water and nature. Slow the heck down. Grow a garden in your house or on your balcony.
Listen to soft music like the soothing sounds of Native American flute! Buy a bicycle and take some rides to nature, or the closest thing to it you can find. Make your

thoughts prayers, by envisioning what you want instead of what you don't want.

Alter your environment as much as you can and encourage others to do so. Start a community garden. Don't be an activist, but act-as-if! Heal your dulled senses slowly by treating them with love. Take relaxing showers and baths, do aroma therapy, and burn sage. Despite the forces around us, try to nurture your senses and bring them back. If you can get to a park, do some communing with nature. Nature heals, so become one with it. Follow animal tracks, notice the plants, shrubs and flowers around you. Learn which plants are edible and medicinal. Talk to nature, trees, animals, and every thing else that is real. Feel the spirit that flows in all things. Don't be a victim, be a spiritual warrior and survivor. Project good imagery in your thoughts. Hey folks this is beyond voting for you favorite guy or gal because you think they will do something for you. This is a spiritual thing so heal your senses, regain your power and project it. Thoughts are strong things, they create and form the world.

Being a Free Spirit

I have often been accused of, and have declared myself as being a "Free Spirit." This can be a blessing or a curse depending on how you look at it. The dictionary defines free spirit as the following: –noun a person with a highly individual or unique attitude, lifestyle, or imagination; nonconformist.

That being said let me try to expound on what being a free spirit means to me, and or how others view it. First, people that are free spirits may have at one time been oppressed or beaten down and vow never to be controlled again. Free spirits may listen and learn from masters, but as Jet Li put it in the movie war, "I have not betrayed my master, because I have no master." The only master they have is the highest one, the flow of life, the universe or the "Tao" because it puts no demands on them, and is non-judgmental and so therefore allows them to be their own master. This means there is no belief in an angry unmerciful type God or entity ready to hail down fire and brimstone. Your concept is more of a higher power or creative force. Your Morality may seem different because of this, because guilt feelings imply bondage, and most likely come from a manipulative attempt.

Creative people are usually free spirits and again maybe people that have been oppressed in the past. You can't trick a free spirit through manipulation, drama, or any other means because since they are free, they see through the bullshit. Sometimes they have studied every means of manipulation you can imagine, including hypnotherapy, religion, and other forms of control like drama from certain relationships, just so they can avoid it.

Now being a free spirit has certain issues that must be recognized. First and foremost is the accusation that they are selfish and care for no one but themselves, and that they are cold. Nothing could be further from the truth. Being a free spirit doesn't mean you don't have compassion for other peoples problems or suffering. As a matter of fact you see these things quite clearly, but prefer non-attachment. How much better it is to help others from that perspective then to get involved in the drama. Being a free spirit means seeing the bigger picture and helping from that view point. Being a free spirit means that at times you find it to the benefit of all concerned to just walk away, or to say no. In the martial arts this is called "The sword of no Sword" Saying no is OK! It's a good thing sometimes. People get mad at free spirits when they walk away or say no because they no longer have control. There is a lot of control issues going around these days. The government wants to control, religion wants to control, your mate, lover, family and so-called friends may want to control, and most times this is done supposedly for your own good. "Free spirits" realize this isn't always true. They usually see the ulterior motives. They listen evaluate and make a decision.

Sometimes being a free spirit allows you to see where other people are in bondage to a way of thinking, and may prompt you to try to help free them in some way. This is the hardest thing of all to a free spirit. Sometimes you are almost willing to sacrifice your freedom to help them, but when push comes to shove if your help or words fall on deaf ears there is nothing you can do except withdraw to keep your own free spirit intact. This doesn't mean you don't love them, in a sense it means you do, because you finally realize they must walk there own path to free spirit status.

Spiritual Tracking & Back Tracking

I Have been going over tom Brown Jr's books lately on tracking. On this read I am seeing applications on a spiritual level. One of the messages that is coming through to me is back tracking or looking at what kind of "life tracks" you have left prior to this moment in time. By analyzing your tracks you can see how you have been walking the path up to this point. When you look at your own track you can see subtleties that can give you clues to the questions that might be cropping up in your life now. Do you feel unbalanced, or maybe indecisive as to the path your on or how to walk that path.

When a good tracker looks at someone's tracks he sees things no one else sees. He might look at a footprint and notice a slightly deeper furrow on one side indicating things such as balance when walking, or maybe the person or animal was lame and favored one foot. If your a really good tracker you can determine how much change is in the guys pockets. So look at your past tracks, in the form of attitudes, missteps, and things that you might have done that brought you to now. Maybe you strayed down a wrong path and suffered a fall, or had to correct course. Maybe you fell a couple of times and didn't learn the right way of walking so as not to fall again. Do you keep stubbing your toe because you refuse to walk softly? There is no sense in walking a walk that doesn't work for us.

By looking at the tracks in our life as a continuum, we can better determine the outcome, or even change it. We can make adjustments to our stride, or maybe walk like a cat instead of an elephant. Maybe we can become more aware of our surroundings, and even our beliefs. Do we believe that there is a monster just around the corner and walk in fear, or are we fearless because we know to handle monsters from past experience. Good trackers are prepared for any contingency so whatever happens can be dealt with in the proper manor.

Be a spiritual tracker as well as a physical one. Study tracking and the ways of nature and apply what you learn to your life on a spiritual level. We can even watch the animals and their tracks and habits, learning from and applying them in our lives. Being in tune with nature and how it effects our nature will put us in oneness with the cosmos and our universal mind. If we get lost in a forest we can always backtrack to find our way out! May your path be filled with joy and wonderment as you traverse the road of life leading to the gateway of the next dimension.

Balance

Balance is about recognizing and knowing intimately the natural forces and energies that flow within and without, and accepting them all equally and with love. When we accept all that is within and love it, all that is without mirrors this acceptance and love. Make something bad within and you are being harsh and judgmental on that part of yourself. Then when you see the reflection of this same thing on the outside, you are judgmental with that. It is all one. When you know and accept yourself, you become a embodiment of the universe and the natural order. Then things begin to flow for you and not against you. It's all about energy. The universe doesn't judge.

The Apache, Warrior, Fighter, Survivor

The Apache was one of the most interesting tribes in my opinion. I highly respect them for many reasons. The Apache was one who certainly lived in harmony with their environment. The desert region they lived in was harsh and unforgiving, particularly regions in the "arid zone" or Arizona. The heat was stifling, and the resources slim, yet they managed to live in perfect harmony with it. Their stealth and warrior ship was unparalleled, as were their stalking and hunting abilities.

Just a side note: I have first hand knowledge of that geographic location having lived there the first sixteen years of my life. I remember days in the summer when the temperatures soared to 110-115 degrees or higher. The nights could get very cold dropping to the extreme. Yet as a boy I walked for miles in bare feet, and trekked and climbed mountains around the surrounding area. This could be one reason I identify with them. When you are raised in a certain location you adapt quickly as a child.

Again most Apaches could do unbelievable things, such as run for miles in extreme heat, sometimes 50 to 80 miles. They could blend so well with the land that they could hide in broad daylight in a sparsely covered desert and not be seen. They could find water and food and often stored it for later. There is a story that goes as follows.

One day a general in the U.S. army asked one of his Indian (Apache) scouts why they couldn't find the band of renegade Apaches they were tracking. The scout answered "because we can hide (Disappear) and not be found, and I can prove it to you." "How so" the general replied." If you turn your back for a few seconds I will hide and you will not find me." The general complied, for he was curious. When he turned back around the scout was no where to be seen. The land was barren except for a tiny scrub brush. He searched the brush and the entire area and was astonished that he was unable to find the scout. In frustration he called out for the scout. Only a few feet away the scout arouse from under the sand, where he had left no marks when he hid away.

This is one reason that the Apache was such an excellent guerrilla fighter. He could spring up out of nowhere, and attack ruthlessly. Most Apaches were crack shots with the repeating rifle or any gun for that matter. They also had an uncanny spiritual connection with what they called the spirits of the land. In the mountains Geronimo hid for many months with a small band, while 5000 soldiers combed the area. They never found him. They say he had spiritual powers, and in fact was never harmed by bullets fired at him or in any skirmishes which were many. He finally surrendered because of the mistreatment of his friends and family.

The Apache scout was the best tracker in the world, just ask Tom Brown Jr. Tom Brown the worlds foremost tracker and survivalist who was trained as a boy by an Apache Indian Named "Stalking wolf" who was in his 80's at the time. Tom was taught to survive in the wilderness with nothing. He could be dropped off in a barren wilderness with no clothes and later come back fully clothed, armed, and well fed. He made all of his clothes, knives, bow, and arrows, out of his surroundings. This is proof of the knowledge that the Apache Stalking Wolf passed on to him.

The Apache clothing was minimal and consisted of nothing more then knee high moccasins a breach cloth, shirt and bandanna to hold back their long hair. They also wore colorful coats, shirts, beads, and jewelry. They didn't have a lot of time for religious practices because most of their time was taken up by survival. Their connection to the spirits were strong though. Their deity was called Usen, and they usually called on the spirits of the land when needing help.

The Apache women were tough also, and were some of the best warriors. One well known woman had the ability to feel on the skin of her arms how many of the enemy were in the area and what their location was. She was also credited with crawling into a Comanche chief's encampment and ripping out his throat with her teeth. She then stole all of his clothes and weapons and brought them back as an offering to her tribe.

Obviously the Apache was feared and respected by the U.S. government. But their fear overcame their respect, and since the Apache was one of the last hold out tribes every effort was made to either exterminate or imprison them. Geronimo himself and all the scouts who worked for the army were shipped off to Florida and imprisoned there. Geronimo never saw his beloved desert home again, and died in an Alabama, reservation under heavy guard in his eighties.

Entertainment vs. Inner Attainment

Sometimes I wonder if all the lengths we go to for entertaining ourselves are really worth the trouble. We live in a world of distraction, some of it purposeful. We baby sit our minds with some type of chattering device like TV and radio, or we have our favorite type of music playing in the background. Then we play with our toys of technology. Is this the Zen of distraction?

A lot of people are in a set routine or rut with their life. This is not entirely their fault, but a product of social conditioning. My father had a saying, a rut is nothing but a grave with both ends knocked out. You might get up, turn on the TV and listen to the latest bad news, while brushing your teeth, or preparing breakfast. Traffic reports, accidents, bad weather, and the same old crap, different day. But lets keep that mind busy with chatter, so we don't hear that small still voice of reason.

Lets just keep on that treadmill of distraction, so we have no time to go to that spirit within. Some people are afraid of their thoughts so they are stuck in that mode of keeping the "bad" thoughts subdued by entertainment. What they don't realize is that the stuff they listen to is probably putting more bad thoughts in their mind. Particularly the bad news, TV, and "commercials" that support our so called entertainment.

So how do we switch from entertainment to inner attainment, the latter being the by-passing of fearful or confusing thoughts and get to the bedrock of spirituality which is silence. One small step at a time that's how. Because if you were to suddenly disconnect from

24

everything that surrounds you it could be a shocking experience. It would be like plunging into a pool of very cold water. My suggestion is this. Try doing without one form of distraction for an hour, a day, or whatever is comfortable for you. Replace it with some form of stillness or meditation, or moving meditation.

Another suggestion would be to slowly, change forms of entertainment to something more calm like reading a good book, one that will perpetuate your goals of inner attainment. Or how about the reconnection to nature and all the natural forms of entertainment which are really a stepping stone to inner attainment? We have myriads of thoughts images and other garbage poured into our mind every day. Why don't we slowly replace or dump out that stuff? Get into creative projects that really make you feel good (god) and give you a sense of peace. Don't just listen to music, play it.

Getting back to the analogy of that pool of cold water. Dip in your toe or foot first and slowly wade in until the pool is no longer a shock but a refreshing change for the better. Disconnect from the illusion of fun and connect with the essence of bliss. Don't condemn yourself for your habits, because they do serve somewhat of a purpose. The way this world is structured we need to have something to keep us from the insanity of everyday life. It's a way to cope and survive. But what is survival if you don't have inner serenity and peace? As wise king Solomon said "it's all a striving after the wind." Make the changes by doing everything in moderation. Even changing to good practices and habits has to be done in moderation.

It's something to think about, food for thought if you will.

Come up with your own ideas and plans on how to do it. Try it you'll like it.

Sitting Bull & His Butterfly Hat

Sitting Bull was a great spiritual visionary, he saw and drew pictures of the Battle of Little Big Horn before they took place. He was a careful man regarding his people who he loved. Some wonder what the significance of the monarch butterfly was on his hat? The butterfly represents transformation and joy, as well as dancing. It is thought that Sitting Bull's butterfly was part of "His Medicine" and his spirit guide. I Know one thing, all of Great Spirit's creatures mean and meant a lot to the Native American way of life. I have always been inspired by the life of Sitting Bull, may he live forever in our Hearts.

Spirits of the Four Directions

To attempt to write on this subject is to walk a fine line and a major undertaking! Why? Because of the personal significance it may have to any one individual, tribe, nation etc. That being said, I am guided to proceed anyway. First there is power in the number four. Four shows up everywhere in Native American culture. It also seems to be a universal number, appearing in other teachings and ritual, like those in the Jewish tradition, particularly the cabala's teaching's of the four angels. Then in the Bible we have Yeshua (Jesus) picking his apostles starting with four, and increasing by four until he has twelve. Twelve being equally divisible by four. Part of the ritual associated with The elders or Pipe Carriers in the Lakota and other traditions is to call upon the Spirits of the Four Directions.

These are as follows Sapa, Luta, Gi, and Okaga Ska. This would be West, North, East and South respectively. The colors being black, red, yellow, and white. Each direction has its own meaning and power. West "Sapa" is a place the thunderbeings (Wakinyan) reside and is considered a place of darkness. This darkness is in a good sense, like that of solitude or meditation and crossing into the spiritual realm. North or "Luta" is a place of renewal and represented by the color red. East "Gi" is a place of brightness, light, clarity and fire with the color being yellow. And South (color white) is a place or door between the spirit world and the visible realm. This circle represents the cycle of life from birth, youth, to elder and death.

Some tribes vary the colors animal representations, and meaning, but one thing for sure, is that the spirits of the four directions are powerful and are waiting to be called upon for direction and help. Walking the wheel of the four directions in this life, can mean you have experienced many cycles of birth and death to former aspects of yourself. This is a natural thing from which we learn lessons and gain wisdom. When we gain enough wisdom we can help others walk the circle and follow ritual. We become elders in a figurative and real sense. Some are called and hear the calling. We carry the pipe, hawk or eagle feather, and drum so we may connect and heal with their use. We use sage a lot along with various other herbs.

Some liken the spirits to the archangels of Michael, Gabriel, Uriel, and Raphael. My own personal take is that these angels have the same properties of the four directions in Native American culture. Uriel is known as the fire of God, and seems to correlate with the thunder beings. Raphael is a healer and could be the same as "Gi" or the spirit of the north who rejuvenates or renews. Gabriel could be the keeper of the spirit world or Okaga ska (South) and Michael can be seen as the rising sun or Son (Clarity) of god. This is my personal vision.

These beings or angels are all beyond gender but all are spiritual warriors, and guides. How often do you call on them to help you walk the Red Road? They all have gifts for you depending on what circumstance you find yourself in. Call on them and they will be by your side instantly. Yes you can even feel them! but you have to respect and honor them by being open minded to their presence. They may send someone to you on the earthly plane, kind of like an undercover angel! Is it real? That's for you to decide. Have you ever had someone appear in your life and say something helpful, and then be gone never to be seen again? All these forces are in unison with Grandfather sky and Grandmother earth which represent the feminine and masculine aspects of the universal mind or spirit.

When loading the sacred pipe, part of the ritual is to say "There is a place in this pipe for you" to each of the directions, and Grandmother and Father. The smoke that rises carries your prayer to Grandfather and all associated with him on a spiritual and earthly level. Don't be surprised to see a hawk or other majestic winged one fly overhead to carry the word. Build yourself a medicine wheel with a colored rock in each of the assigned four directions. Buy the books "The Sacred Pipe" by Black Elk or "Seeker of Visions by Lame deer." Become an apprentice to the tried and true ways of old. Also, I might mention that the colors Black, yellow, Red, and White represent the colors or races of mankind working as one, or being one. All my relations! The original inhabitants were called "Human Beings," or people of the earth, because they lived in harmony with it. There are no wannabees, there are only those who are and those who are not walking the Red Road regardless of race. If you like, you can call it the good road, or earth road but I call it red because red represents renewal and rebirth.

But all man or two leggeds along with the four leggeds, winged ones, and plant life are all related. We are all one. All my relations! My writings and words are for many purposes some apparent and some not so apparent, but spirit asks and I write. It is good. Hecheto welo.

Giving & Receiving

I have recently had the privilege to experience generosity, support, and donations from various people, who have received benefit from my thoughts and council. I want to thank them! Some have been through incredible adversity. For the record, adversity sometimes brings out the best in people. The times are trying, and situations difficult. I am very happy people have been contacting me for an exchange of healing energy. Their donations and support allow me to help them and others, but I always will and have helped, regardless.

The nation and world finds itself in circumstances that are putting a lot of pressure on the "family" of man in general. And that is exactly what we all are, "family!" Those who are "perceptive" on a spiritual level realize that the current monetary situation which has and will affect us all, is an awakening of sorts.

This awakening comes through the realization that the pursuit of money (the green frog skin) is not what this existence is all about. Greed and living the so-called high life at the expense of others has opened a Pandora's box, and is bringing realization and enlightenment regarding what is really important in life. Just because the people in power have created chaos by their greed, doesn't mean that we as "The family"(all of my relations) have to follow suit.

This is the very time when we should realize that the tradition of the "give-away" in Native American tradition is exactly what is going to heal and help all concerned. Giving comes in many forms. Giving of love, compassion and understanding, and sharing on a monetary level. We

31

need to all "hold hands" and walk the "Red Road" together.

Its amazing to me that the media and others keep bombarding us with bad news and negativity on the one hand, while on the other they are still trying to tell us to go out & pursue the temporary fix of material mind excitation. The talking heads tell us how bad and dire things are, and the commercials tell us to go out and take a trip to the Caribbean, or buy the latest S.U.V. or other pricey possession.

The whole system is based on the rich riding on the backs of the poor. Go out and work hard, pay your taxes, and stay on the treadmill, and then lose everything including your retirement, house, and nest egg in a blink of an eye. This was never intended for us by great spirit. The intention was for us to live in accordance with Grandmother Earth and to receive her bounty. Each man should have, or "live under his own vine and fig tree."

So what do we do now? We ban together and form circles of friends who re-establish the practice of the natural order of life. We should give from the heart and we will receive from Great Spirit, through others. Give possessions, love, or just good thoughts to others. It feels damn good and is a healing in itself. Its no wonder things are the way they are when some relinquish their personal power, spirit, and soul, to those who have no soul. I have enormous empathy for my brothers and sisters suffering. It doesn't help to be stuck in the anger mode at those who may have caused this mess, or ourselves for buying into it. Love is required and necessary all the way around. Look at this as an event that could be the best thing that ever happened.

Start today, and experience the incredible good feelings linked to the experience of giving, loving, and feeling compassion for others. There is nothing in this world that we can take with us into the next except our spiritual evolution. I will continue to give to others through my writing energy, and whatever else I can come up with. I just want you all to know that I am thankful for your trust, and positive energy in whatever form it takes. The fact that you read and consider my thoughts, helps me fulfill what I consider to be my purpose in life.

The Drum Circle

I went to the park today with the intention of seeing if the sick rabbit I found the other day was OK! I had done a little feather ritual on it the day before. He was gone so he is either OK, or crawled away somewhere! Hopefully he is healed. As I was sitting in my sacred space in the thick foliage, something directed my steps up the hill. I heard drums in the distance. Am I having a vision? I started to walk toward the sounds, and as I got closer I saw that it was a drum circle with at least 10 to 15 drummers. All kinds of people with various drums. I had my staff and walked closer in. I started chanting and pounding my staff on the ground. I got good vibes so I chanted louder "Mitakuye Oyasin. Hi ye yoh hey yoh hey hey!" The vibe picked up. There was a drum sitting on the edge of the circle. I gravitated toward it. It was huge! it was a thunder drum! It was 4 ft tall by at least 12 to 13 inches wide. It looked African! A fellow close by, told me to play it. I fell into the cacophony of rhythms. I laid done a tribal riff using my left hand with clenched fist (boom) and my right open palm slapping in alternate strokes. The ground was literally shaking. I increased my chanting and playing. The drummers were all one with me increasing the rhythm to a fever pitch. I knew none of these people, but yet I knew them all...They were all my relations, There were women, children, Anglos, Hippies, Hispanics, Native Americans, old, young, and a guy in a wheel chair. There were all kinds of drums, rattles, and shakers. The more I chanted the more the excitement increased. People were going tribal, women, children, and men were dancing in the middle. I played for two maybe three hours full on. As I left one of the lead drummers shook my hand and said what's your name, I'm Thunderhands, some call me Thunder. He had a big smile, and said come back next Sunday. I was exhausted!!...I floated home. As I was walking home two hawks flew overhead. When I got home I threw the I-Ching (Chinese Oracle) and it came up with two hexagrams. Number two "The Creative" and number eight "holding together" or "creating union with others." Does it get better then this?....I had to write this! This is a true story! Only the names have been changed to protect the innocent. (laughs) Feb 22?... 22 is my numerological number. 22/4

A Song of Healing

I am a spiritual being in a divine universe.
All events and lessons in life are for my benefit.
I have reverence and gratitude for all that is.
I am quiet, still, and calm, while retaining presence of mind.
I use all perceived adversity to gain strength.
I choose to walk the Red Road of goodness.
I ask and allow the Great Spirit that moves in all things, to move through and with me, for illumination on the path.
I am one with this universal spirit of healing energy.
I accept the healing, compassion, and love received, and share it with all creation in heaven and earth. To the winged ones, the two and four legged, Grandmother earth and Grandfather sky.
I am a positive participant in the circle of life.
I walk the medicine wheel, with all my relations.
Mitakuye Oyasin

Transforming Hate into Love

When you hate another, the hatred will consume you until you become captivated by it. In a sense you become the hated and take on their persona. Sometimes this will lead you into the realization that they are none other then yourself, because we are all one.

What you hate you must love, which brings about a transformation, and rebirth. If you continue to hate, you are hating yourself, which brings grief to your spirit. This brings about confusion and leads to self destructive tendencies. Why hate when you can love? Love feels Good (god) and is in alignment with, or feeds off of spirit or higher self.

To love is to bring balance to your soul and a clarity and purpose to your life. It elevates you towards the higher plateau called enlightenment, and sets your moccasins on the right path.

Don't make hate an enemy but see it as an opportunity or sign, to shape shift into love. "It's all about energy." When hate is directed your way you may not feel it, or notice it, (unless your highly attuned) because of the way it can be masked. So practice being in a loving space, and having a loving aura or energy field. This will set up a protective barrier which will repel or transmute any negative energy into light. Then the person projecting hate will get a bounce back of love instantly.

This is a way we heal our fellow man and protect ourselves. With a transformation and redirection of energy.

What your Reality Can Teach You

Let your reality be bio feedback for your spirit. How much
of your mind is physical or carnal, and how much is spirit?
Let objects that surround you, remind you of your different
sides. Everything is a reflection of you. All situations,
objects, friends and family. The clutter in your house, the
sounds outside, everything.

What you see, hear, and feel indicate what your mind is
projecting onto the field of phenomenon in this illusion or
dream (Maya) we call life. Let your higher self reflect
through your mind more clearly by removing thoughts and
preconceptions. Give objects outside of yourself a power or
meaning that will enable your spirit.

Does that statue you have of Quan Yin really make you feel
the compassion and mercy of the feminine side of the
universal mind, or does it just sit there like a lump of clay
or pottery?

Even what people say could be you, projecting thoughts on
them. Imagine what the world would look, sound, and feel
like if your mind was no mind and pure spirit. Would you
see everything as crystalline, and with an aura of energy?
Would your environment be more natural and less man
made? When you look at the picture of life what comes to
mind? Could you re-frame the picture so that it appeals to
or feeds your spirit.

What wolf do you feed the spirit wolf or the carnal wolf?
Feed the spirit wolf, more and the carnal wolf less, or just
enough to keep one foot in the physical world while you
are really walking in the spiritual. Your mind is like an

auto-pilot programmed from birth. Take it off the programmed mode and push the clear button, and from this moment on let spirit be the program for your auto-pilot. Let the universal mind guide you to the friendly skies, and fly united with the spirit that moves in all things.

Ride above yourself and watch your body and world from a higher place where the red tailed hawks fly. Ride on the wave of the ultimate ocean of spirit, and pure wisdom. Become a vessel for the creative energy to flow into. Being receptive is embracing the goddess energy. Be the little yin in the big Yang, (see yin yang sign) and the little yang in the big yin. Let the balance which is inherent, or our true nature be evident in our life.

You will still have lessons to learn, but not be overwhelmed. The lessons become easier as we become more refined and balanced. The more you temper the sword of the spirit the sharper it becomes. This will allow you to cut through the obstacles that appear in your life like a hot knife through butter. Remember let your surroundings have meanings that empower you and you will notice a paradigm shift.

The Heart Flower Poem

The Thunder rolls and Lightening strikes and sometimes
our life seems dire.
But just open your hearts and let others in, its like kindling
for a fire.
The fire brings warmth and plenty of joy, and causes the
miracle of light.
And with this miracle comes a chain reaction, causing spirit
to grow so bright.
If you let the fire consume your fears, and burn up thoughts
that don't empower.
Out of the ashes grows a thing called love, which is a like
beautiful flower.

The Plainsmen & The Indians

Plainsmen is a generalized term that could and does encompass a lot of characters. Anyone who had the grit made their way out into the great plains, deserts, and forest, of early America, Canada, and parts of Mexico. Don't look for the fainthearted in this bunch. You have everyone from Daniel Boone to wild Bill Hickok. There were drifters, gold miners, trappers, mountain men, cowboys, gunslingers, and the strong stouthearted women who accompanied, or serviced them in some way. Even General Custer in the earlier years put up a defense for, and learned from the "savages" at times. There were the immigrants and cattle barons, the railroaders and sod busters and just a general mass of people looking for a better life.

It was a colorful time, when people lived hard, next to the land, and fought harsh environments. But you can imagine what the thoughts of the original inhabitants of this country were. A land that was pristine was soon over run by all of the above. Many of the tribes tried to cope in a peaceful way but soon realized that this was all but futile, as the white man in general spoke with a forked tongue. Still the real true mountain men and plainsmen looked to bridge the gap, and learn from the aboriginal people of the earth about their ways. There was an inclusion of many customs, hunting techniques and dress from the native tribes of the different regions. Scouts and trackers learned their skills from the very people they were later to hunt down. The Red Man was willing to share and live together in many instances until their back was against the wall.

The white man and the United States government owe these people a huge debt. If they had tried to become one with the land, and learned how to integrate with it, we wouldn't have the problems we are facing today. But greed got the better of most, with money, gold, and land grabbing being the order of the day. Still the Native American spirit is strong and many of, if not most of our states and cities are named after tribes, and people that were the original inhabitants. All in all it was a colorful time, and a part of history. But looking back, my sentiments of course are with the "people of the earth" and those who reached out to them by trying to learn their ways. Some even lived with them and became mixed blood. Many today are waking up to the true nature of these spiritual people and what they still might have to offer.

And what is really interesting is that their blood line extends or flows in many of the people living in the America's until this day.

Loving Yourself

Means rejoicing in the fact that you are a special person with all your perceived faults or flaws. Do you accept and embrace your shadow side or "Nagi" as it is called in the Lakota language. Do you realize that you are special and that there is no one quite like you on the planet. Do you look in the mirror and say I love and accept you.

What reason would there be not to think that you are as much a child of the universe, God, Great Spirit or whatever you call the Deity as the next person. I was telling a friend that I sometimes felt bad about the way some people might view me, or missed the point of my thoughts and writings, and if I was communicating in a way that could help others. His reply was "I haven't seen any perfect people walking the earth Lately, and what about all the people that send you those heart warming letters."

I agree with the Zen viewpoint that we are all potential Buddha's or Christ's, but we all are colored by our social conditioning, and thoughts from outside sources implanted in us since childhood. This can cause fragmentation or not being in harmony with the self. Does this mean that we should reject ourselves? Maybe we don't feel as spiritual or successful as the next guy. Does that mean we are worthless? The answer is no.

Life's lessons are valuable and can teach us how to rely on the connection with our higher self. We all are miracles, and life itself is a miracle. Don't sell yourself short. There is an old movie with Jimmy Stewart called "Its a wonderful life." He is taken off the planet as if he never existed, and the effect on his family and the community was sad and devastating because of the loss of his presence. This just means that we may affect people in ways we never dreamed of. It means that we all have something to give. It means we have the ability to change the planet and other peoples lives for the better. Yes us! Little old me and you.

It is important to remember that when we do things that we don't like, it serves as a signpost to change course. Sometimes this can't be done overnight. After all it took us years to get to where we are. Life is a journey, change comes quicker when we don't force things, and acquire a healthy dose of acceptance. Just like the tide slowly erodes the cliff we need to be like water. Mind like water, letting bad thoughts flow away. Yes be like water, slowly wearing away your perceived bad character traits or habits, forgiving yourself when we don't instantly correct course.

Forgive yourself and others when you are disappointed. Don't carry the burden by yourself, love is all around you but sometimes you can't see it or feel it. Quite the mind and still the thoughts and feel the power of it, knowing that you and it are one, and that you are always loved. Cast off the feelings of not being worthy, for when you were a child you knew that you were. Regain the innocence of a babe, and rejoice in your own foot or hand, or the reflection of yourself in the mirror.

Throw away the rule book, it's the spirit, not the law. When you begin to love yourself you find it easier to love others, and them you. When you do something good remember it. Its so easy to forget the good things we do. We are all that little boy, or girl of innocence. It's just that we have been hurt along the way. Throw the hurt away and live life for another day.

What is Love?

Have you ever thought about love and how sometimes it is hard to describe. I have many feelings that are about love. Usually the question of it comes up when there is a lack of love in your own life, or when what you expect of others and sometimes ourselves, fails to manifest itself. So as I was thinking about love, a myriad of things started flowing into my mind. Believe me I think the Bible writers even wrestled with what love was, even though they tried to spell it out. Here are some thoughts that came up that could or could not be love, but are maybe extensions of it. Also things came up that were not love, things related to love etc. I will write you decide if it helps your definition. Finally Love is just a word, its the "feeling" that counts. Admittedly you can't cure all of the world's ills, but you can start small, within your own circle of friends and family and work your way out.

Love is when a soldier throws his body on a live grenade to save his fellow man.

Love is seeing a homeless person not as disgusting, or a bum, but as a part of yourself that needs help.

Love is a mother instinctively holding her child to her breast to provide nourishment and nurturing.

Love is sometimes erotic.

Love is hugging your fellow man or woman.

Love is seeing the look in your pet's eyes, when it is hungry or needs to go out, and you take care of it immediately.

Love comes easy for animals and hard for humans

Love is seeing the look in your fellow man's eyes when he is hungry or needs the basic comforts of life, and not turning your back.

Love is anticipation of things needed by others, and giving it to them before they have to ask, or are afraid to.

Love is a four letter word for something hard to explain, but you know it when you feel it, or give it.

Loving is reaching inside, to reach outside.

Love is not making your fellowman, friend, or family member beg you for love, and or help.

Love is forgiving your fellowman, friend, or family member when they don't give you love or help, when you need it.

Love is not passing by someone in need and turning your head the other way.

Love is not using catch phrases like "I love You" or "Love from so and so," and not showing it with some type of demonstrable action.

Love is seeing all mankind as one with yourself, having empathy for their condition, and making some kind of physical or spiritual effort to change it for the better.

Love is forgiving others as many times is as needed.

Love is not giving up on others.

Love is not giving up on yourself.

Love is not judging others by our own egotistical standards, turning your back on them, or casting them out of your circle or from society.

Love is acceptance of others lifestyle, and personal choices without condemnation.

Love is tolerance of others spiritual beliefs

Love is not trying to force your beliefs on others.

Love is saying and meaning "you don't have to pay me back."

Love comes from the heart, and never ends.

Love is a state of being.

Love is compassion, mercy, and forgiveness of ourselves and others.

Love is saying don't worry about it, I got it!

Love is enabling not disabling.

Love is seeing all others as Family.

Love is making room for others when there is no more room.

Love is feeling lighter when you give, and heavier when you don't.

Love is considering how our words and actions might affect others.

Love is knowing that one act of kindness toward another could change our whole life and the their life too.

Love is not reading into someone's words or tone of voice something bad, but giving them the benefit of the doubt.

Love is something that can come through you and to others from the universal mind, and return to you from others.

Love is something that requires nothing other then opening up your heart to it.

Love given from the heart feels damn good to give and receive, and is healing.

Love not given from the heart, but out of guilt, or a sense of obligation, is not love.

Love doesn't give out of self righteousness.

Love lifts the spirit of the giver and receiver.

Love is a feeling, and an energy.

Love is not taking credit for things but giving credit to

others, or to the source of all good things.

Love should be given at any time under any condition.

Love heals giver and receiver.

Love is what you see in your fellowman's eyes when you love him.

I think I could go on forever, or for a very long time, but in case my words didn't cover it all (And I didn't) then maybe these will.

A very wise man once said "Treat others they way you would want to be treated" and "Love Your neighbor as yourself."
Notice it says love yourself, which is a presumption that you should be.

The Zen Teachings of Jesus (Yeshua)

When Jesus spoke of the child, and becoming as a child, he was very much in line with Zen thought. We lose the virtue of the child mind as we gain greater dependence on spoken language and become more aware of the world. As a result of outside controls which are introduced by words and enforced by some type of threat, we begin to trust our own instincts less, with the result being the creation of a dualistic mind. Many of us also lose that sense of self worth.

This divides the inner from the outer, me from you, and in the larger sense good from evil, etc. The young child's mind is like a clear glass of water that becomes polluted with external worldly rules, concepts, dogma, and societal conditioning in general. We eventually loose touch with that kingdom within.

The Zen term of "Mushin" refers to original mind, empty mind, or "Child's Mind." We are born enlightened and spend our whole life trying to get back to that state of mind. guilt, fear, anger and a lot of negative emotions come from indoctrination and a muddying of the water. Its no wonder that Christ said "Unless you become as a child you shall not see the kingdom of God." Couple that with his words of "The Kingdom of Heaven is within you" and you have one of the most advanced Zen teachings known.

Is Jesus a Zen master, or are Zen masters exemplars of Christ? It matters not, for universal law is universal law. Jesus was an enlightened being, or master. Master of himself, master of the universe and teacher of "The Way." Christians who worship or go to church but don't catch the true meaning behind his words, and fail to even try to comprehend what he was teaching, are just going through the paces. Worse yet they may be projecting belief systems that are diametrically opposed to what Yeshua stood for. I guess that's why we should heed the admonition of "being aware of false prophets." or 'Wolves in sheep's clothing." This not to say there are no "sincere Christian's."

It is not for me to judge. However most Christian religions, and churches indoctrinate and lay guilt on people, as well as causing a lot of hate and fear. This is not conducive to having a child's mind as spoken about by "Yeshua." Why follow empty rhetoric and dogmatic teachings, when you can go directly to the source and receive direct transmission.

My Prayer to Earth Mother

Earth mother, you are the sacred feminine, the female aspect of the universe. Open your arms and embrace me. Send the healing force of nature to be my companion. Raise my spirit with your nurturing presence. Guide my feet as I walk on your fertile ground. Unite me with the "Spirit" that moves in all things. Show me the path of "The Red Road." Balance my body mind and soul, and ground me in your love, mercy, and compassion. Give me the strength to move upward like a seedling making it's way to the sun. Calm and clear my mind like the surface of a smooth pond. Give me a firm foundation like the majestic mountains that endure through the ages. Make my heart soft like the snowflakes that fall from the misty clouds of your breath. Protect and shelter me like a bear in its cave of hibernation. Renew me like the cherry blossoms of spring. I honor you for your wisdom and thank you for it. May I be one with all that is your creation.

Trust & Gratitude

Sometimes we just have to trust the higher power, our higher selves, or great spirit, for guidance. Times can be really tough, and events can trigger us into feeling down or unhappy. When we are in these situations we try everything we can to advance correctness, but sometimes we run into obstacles. To put it simply we try too hard. When faced with this situation retreat and take a rest. Give it up to the higher power for a while, with trust that it will work out.

If possible keep the ego uninvolved, by stilling restless thoughts. Once we identify something that needs to be corrected in ourselves or others, gentle but ceaseless penetration is the key. Like the wind blowing steadily in the same direction wearing away doubts, and inferior ego driven qualities.

At times of darkness, gratitude for all the good things in your life can bring in some light. Just remember that you are one with the higher power who embodies the father, mother and eternal love. You have spiritual help all around you, and it doesn't hurt to ask or pray for help. Don't try to do it all yourself. Let go of any dark thoughts and aggressive attempts to make things right. Be grateful for the lessons that can redirect your path to a more beneficial outcome.

Surviving the World's Perfect Storm

A high percentage of souls in the world right now are angry, scared, and apprehensive about the future. Anger, fear, and other negative emotions abound everywhere. There seems to be an overwhelming amount of pressure on the inhabitants of this wonderful planet earth. You might even call it a world wide perfect storm. An analogy might be the movie called "The Perfect Storm" in which a series of meteorological events caused a horrendous, and destructive storm. The series of events happening in this world right now have reached this high magnitude. An aware person certainly might ponder the outcome, and wonder what they can do to "Ride this one out."

The elements that make up the storm can be summed up largely with three words "Decrease, Opposition, and Return." Let's take the first element of "Decrease." We see significant evidence of decrease in all area's of life. The financial global markets are to put it bluntly, crashing. This causes a decrease in all of the other areas, a domino effect if you will. One of the domino's is a decrease in tolerance, which results in anger and fear. Another component of this perfect storm is the political climate, which by a strange twist of fate is happening at the same time as the decrease. The world political climate can be considered a component of "opposition." This opposition is fueling the fire of anger, hatred, racism, and religious intolerance. This is done by stirring up our most basic and primal fears of anyone who might be considered different, or a threat to our survival. The third element of the storm "return" is cyclical change. Change is a fact of life, but this cyclical change, is the ending of the old and the beginning of the new.

Now the "Decrease" part of the storm can be largely attributable to the souls who inhabit this planet, and live in this world. Decrease comes when there is too much increase, a re-balancing if you will. The increase we are talking about in this instance was an increase in the egotistical elements, of greed, false pride, and materialism. The "Opposition" element is connected with the political, ideological, and religious (not spiritual) components of our world, and is showing itself in very ugly and angry ways. Again we have the emotion of "anger" being a particularly destructive component of this storm.

Lets talk about the element of "Return" or cyclical change for a moment. In a normal world and planet, this is a natural thing and takes different forms. However because of the aforementioned components of greed, false pride, and materialism, the planet may be forced into a premature or early cyclical change, called global warming. The greenhouse effect, global warming, and pollution of the planet, are all the results of the self centered thought "grab all you can, while you can." This attitude of the powers to be, or the worlds leaders, is without regard to our natural habitat. The rich get richer (materialism) and the earth suffers in return. The good people on the planet who have mistakenly put their faith, future, and protection in other' people's hands, are having a rude awakening right now. The result being more anger and fear.

It isn't a very cheery scenario, or picture I know. But there are measures that you can take to protect your sanity, and remained centered and calm. In fact if you look at the situation from a different point of view, you have the possibility to emerge from this period of time, stronger, healthier, and wiser. How? You may ask.

55

Again I will use the analogy of the storm, "Batten down the Hatches." What does this mean in real terms? Simply this, "Go Within." When they batten down the hatches on a ship they go within for protection. Your goal should be to stay in the eye of the hurricane and not the wall. The "I-Ching" an ancient Chinese Oracle, has all of the aforementioned terms of Opposition, Decrease, and Return, as names for hexagrams (64 in all) of cyclical change, and phases we may experience.

The "I-ching" is like receiving advice from a wise master, your higher self or the deity of your choice. In times of decrease it advises us to "be still, lessen the power of the ego and misfortune will be avoided." When our resources are limited and difficulty surrounds us, our egos generate angry and unhappy emotions. This also happens when we are unable to achieve our goals. In the current political climate this is evident. One side may think that their ship is going down and their ego's become infuriated. This hardens them so much that they propagate and display anger and bitterness. Also because of this intense world situation, in most peoples lives this same scenario and reaction is taking place. In other words, they find opposition affecting them and their relationship with others. Do you see what I mean by the perfect storm?

Take the advice of the wise sage. Be still, meditate, and "return" to your quiet center, like a spring returns to the inside of a mountain during a time of drought.
Withdraw from the media, newspapers, and negative influences. If you find yourself screaming at someone on TV, turn it off. Sacrifice the ego, for it is powerless against the currents of life. You can't force progress by arguing,

manipulation, or making excuses. In a sense you are retreating to the calm eye of the hurricane, instead of getting caught in the wall, and are flowing with the storm until it dissipates.

The "I-ching" or sage also speaks of this opposition, quote: "Misunderstanding truth creates opposition." you might add "distorting truth" to this also. It speaks of events in life, which can tempt us into negative thoughts and mistrust of others. It can cause us to mistrust life, and believe that it is working against us. The lessons that we and the planet as a whole are experiencing, are lessons that we need at this time in our evolutionary process or journey. Whatever is happening now must happen. We can't resist, because even if we try we can't prevent the progress of cyclical changes that must take place. Its time to display our higher and more loving aspects of ourselves. Transmute the anger and hatred to love, and let go of dark thoughts and aggressive actions. Embody the sage, Jesus, or some other high spiritual person or purpose that is your ideal. It's time to strengthen your inner light and reserves.

The I-ching's comments about "Return" offer a positive possibility to this story. It says: "A time of darkness comes to an end." This is a turning point, the greatest adversity can be put behind us and the light can return. It warns that it can't be forced, and so you might as well rest and act only when you can move gently and innocently. Return also means to return to the light within yourself. Growth is only possible when we relinquish the expressions of the ego: Pride, impatience, anger and desire. Let things develop naturally in their own way. "Simply observe and accept changes as you observe and accept the rising of the sun." Gather your strength for a new growth ahead, and a return to the light. It's up to you as an individual and all of us collectively to change our consciousnesses, or it will be changed for us.

Life is a Journey

Like a good friend said to me today. "It's not the negatives and the positives that define life, they might make life more interesting, and bring out different aspects, but its all about the journey." We truly are wanderers or travelers on this road we call life. The bumps in the road definitely push us toward a more reflective mode. But no matter what comes our way we have to be flexible and flow around the obstacles, instead of beating our head against them. It's this allowing the flow of the river to push us along, that puts us in touch with the Tao and Great Spirit. When I was a pilot and flight instructor, the first instinct when you hit turbulence is to fight it. But the best method to get out of that situation, is not to fight it or panic. It's funny how not fighting things works better then fighting. It all about resistance. Just like electricity flowing through a wire. The wire causes resistance and stops the energy from flowing as freely. But when lightening come from the sky there is no resistance. Let your life be without resistance to the natural energy, or chi surrounding us and life in general. Be like lightening. And walk what the Native American calls the "Red Road."

The Suffering of the Masses

I can't let this current financial situation go by without
commenting more on it. It seems history has lessons for us
if we look for them. Any empire is vulnerable, when the
focus of it's agenda is on the material instead of the
spiritual. America has been walking a thin line for a long
time. Greed and power is the name of the game. It's a form
of gluttony.

It's been that way since day one, when the Peaceful Native
American inhabitants of this beautiful land, were
eliminated to a large degree by a form of genocide. If you
believe in karma, then its being delivered in large portions.

The American public are not graduates from an elite school
of finances and are in the dark about the intricacies of how
the system works or doesn't work. They are depending on
the chiefs of the tribe called the government to watch over
and protect them. Now in contrast, you have the Indian
chiefs of the Native American tribes, who were allowed to
be in their position because they proved themselves to be
honorable men through years of observation by the rest of
the tribe. Where are the honorable men in our society? How
do we know who is honorable and who isn't?

A couple of quotes from different traditions are in order.
"When the evil are in power the people suffer" (I-ching)
"By their fruits you shall know them" (Bible) "Certainly
they are a heartless nation, they have made some of their
people servants" "The greatest objects of their lives seems
to be to acquire possessions-to be rich." "They desire to
possess the whole world." (White Footprint- Sioux).

60

The majority of American people try to do the right thing, but it seems they face oppression, panic and fear at every turn of the road, and are in fact slaves. They work hard to just survive, while the leaders of the land they live in gorge themselves on the fruits of the peoples labor. This problem is deep and systemic. The American people have a gut feeling that something isn't right. And the feeling is something they should follow, it's called intuition. There are no quick fixes to something of this nature.

It is better to take no action then the wrong action, or an action that is meaningless. I won't take sides regarding the political situation, but know this. These people (government leaders) are not stupid, they are deep into military strategy, and know how to manipulate and distract the masses of people. We don't really know the inner workings of their minds other then what we can see by the results that are evident.

I would be presumptuous to claim to have the answers, but here is a thought that I have repeated often. Since we seem to be in a position where we have no real control other then to speak out. Try to remain calm, centered and detached, because if there is anything that these people want, its for you to panic so that you can be manipulated through your fear. Keep a clear head, and connect with people of like mind who know that this isn't right. We the people are collectively stronger then those who lead. Its time to band together on many levels including the spiritual. Meanwhile the commercials wail on about all the material things we just must have now! Welcome to the reservation.

People in Panic

Earlier in my some of my writings I talked about being of the world but not in it. "The world" is in a panic about money and the economy. What does it say when people feel the need to e-mail the media and ask them what to do? What's needed is a spiritual perspective on the ebb and flow of life, including money and material things. With the majority of people in this life having some form of religious or spiritual upbringing, this question begs to be answered. Why do they depend so much on government (political figures), and the media, to supply them with consolation and or protection? Have these entities become their God. Their is no solace in taking refuge in a house that is falling apart.

Just a few key words and phrases come to mind from various spiritual traditions. Don't store up your treasures where rust and moths can consume them. Practice non-attachment to everything including your own body on a daily basis, or at least think about it. The Tao Te Ching speaks of change and cycles and how inevitable these things are. The time has come to ask if your are watching this from a detached position or are you getting caught up in a struggle against inevitability's. Making the government, the media, and even external religions your basis for protection and spiritual solace is maybe not the best approach. We all are tempted to get caught up in the vicissitudes of life, yours truly included. In a nutshell this make things more painful. The government, media, and religion are like the wizard of Oz. Much ado about nothing. In other words for all practical purposes, look behind the face they are wearing.

Has past history indicated anything other then propagation of falsehood, lies and deceit? Is this something you can count on when the chips are down? The bottom line is to start today with a new realization, and that is that everything you need is within you. Look inside not outside. The kingdom of heaven is within, if you will. Meditation, prayer, and genuine reflection are my recommendation. Go to the well of spirituality and solace within, because out in the world promises made are not promises kept. My prayers and thoughts are with my fellow man, and my hopes are that this will be an awakening of some sort as to what the real priorities are in life. Don't get caught up in "Maya" or the illusion we call life.

The Feminine aspect of the Universe & The Tao

I love the goddess aspect of the universe. The Tao Te Ching says: "It (the Tao) is the unlimited father and mother of all limited things" Picture two photos of the goddess aspect being portrayed. One with the dragon (Taoist) and the other with the Thunderbird or thunder beings (Native American). We also have many other examples, such as Kwan Yin goddess of mercy, and the White Buffalo Woman who gave the Native American the red stone pipe. Grandmother or mother earth comes to mind also. Certainly these cultures realized the importance of the soft and yielding manner of the "Yin energy." With this comes the gift of compassion and mercy. It would be beneficial for any society, especially those of a patriarchal nature to recognize and embrace the dual aspect of nature and the universe. This should also be recognized within oneself. Another quote from The Tao Te Ching of Lao Tzu: "To know the masculine and yet cleave to the feminine is to be the womb of the world." Needless to say we could use a more soft yielding atmosphere in the world we see around us.

Gods Goddesses & Deities

Just what are these God's and or archetypes if you will, and where do they come from. If you asked Joseph Campbell (worlds foremost authority on mythology) he would say that Gods, Goddesses, deities, are something that men, women, tribes, and cultures, in different periods of time created or manifested through their connection to the collective unconscious.

So in my way of thinking. The Greeks have Thor, the Jews Yahweh, the Chinese a pantheon of God, Goddesses. They again were thought of, and or infused into an existing real person. Things become legend and take on a life of their own. So to make a long story short. We (mankind) created gods or aspects of the one universal force or the Tao, because it (The Tao) can't be named. These creations or gods are us really, or aspects of ourselves or higher selves. How real can they become? Maybe as real as we want or need them to be. For instance if a deity or God or immortal such as Kwan Kun was created for protection. Then maybe that thought perpetuated over thousands of years has quite a bit of power. Of course anything has as much power as you want to give it also. So with those thoughts in mind maybe we should use these external projections to our advantage like we do with the immortals of feng shui.

In a sense it is a universal mind game on a high level. What's fascinating to me is many of these Gods or Goddesses appear in similar forms or exact forms from cultures or peoples that never knew each other. So it has to come from the collective unconscious. Now the question arises what is this collective unconscious. Even Campbell didn't claim to know really. Is it the great mystery? The Tao? The Great Spirit that moves in all things? Yes, that's my best guess. I would like to think that it is projecting these myths and archetypes on us for our benefit. Feng shui is common sense, (geomancy) a science. But it is a belief system too. Its good to believe in a protecting deity or guardian. The mind is powerful and can use the imagery of that God for our benefit.

Healing & Addictive Thinking

The ego may feel threatened if it was to not have this addictive thread or compulsion. On the other hand your true self may feel a whole lot better if you didn't have this way of thinking coloring the world. It would be like lifting a burden from your shoulders and removing something that might be blocking an energy channel in your aura. This could then even be manifesting as that sensation in your physical being. Letting go of this thread of preconditioning could free you of tension in your body.

Is this going to be a difficult thing ridding yourself of this thinking addiction? Maybe it boils down to this. How difficult do you want it to be? Sometimes you might have to form an alliance with your ego and higher self. Make an agreement that you will be gentle with the ego. Don't start a war within yourself. Make a bridge between the ego and your higher self or "sage" self. All relationships take time to develop. Should the one within be any different? Work with it at your own speed. As you continue this "awareness in the moment" process, as time goes on things become easier. You begin to see more clearly the patterns of addictive thought. You begin to see a cause and effect. Not with just thinking, but with your physical addictions as well.

Just remember as you practice this awareness process, not to judge, condemn, or beat yourself up. Chances are that whatever it is that is manifesting in your life that's not serving your best interests, might have come from a lack of compassion or love in the first place. So give yourself plenty of love. This is a good way to heal and become enlightened in the process. To me, being enlightened is removing the heavy load and becoming a lighter being, or light being. So ponder these thoughts, and begin a new journey as a wanderer and wonderer of life. Make this the first day of a new healing journey and a new life. The life you really want.

In the world but not of it

This thought is kind of an extension of previous thought, and could be an ongoing topic, but I don't think that far ahead. Reading my previous writings might give you a little more insight into this one.

So continuing on the premise that we are a product of social conditioning since birth, from all the input of the "world" around us. And that this is what created our ego, and all our supposed wants and needs. Lets look at our thinking, and the possibilities surrounding that process. As we live in the awareness of the moment we notice thoughts arising about our experience. And as we look or reflect on these thoughts, while viewing the flow of them with no judgment. We start getting closer to our "essence" by realization.

We should have a "wondering attitude" about what is creating our feelings, sensations, and thoughts about the present moment. Pictures or images may arise from what's coming up. Again let these images come gently, like bubbles rising to the surface of a pond. You might have a sudden awakening. You could see things that astound you. You might even say things like, Wow! now I see why I feel this way about what I am experiencing. You might see an incident in your life that is triggering the emotional response your having at the moment. Sensations, could arise in your body. Whether they are pleasurable or not, let thoughts about them float to the surface. Are you causing this pleasure or pain because of an earlier event?

Suppose you say yes, an event happened when I was 12 years old. The question then arises. But how could that event have anything to do with my preconditioning, I wasn't in my formative years? OK, so take that event and trace it back further. Don't force it just let it happen. As you trace this "thread" back, (and this could happen all in just a few moments or minutes) you begin to see that there might be a pattern of addictive thinking, or a "series" of events. The real kicker comes when you have a vision of what might have been the original stimuli that caused this thread of events, and or addictive thinking. You might also see how that this pattern is something that became part of the ego. It might be such an entrenched part of your ego, that it (your ego) makes you feel like you need to keep it.

I have been thinking about the phrase "In the world but not of it." Where did this thought come from and what does it mean to you and I? First, let me start by saying that the thought has been around for a long, long, time and is found in many ancient wisdom traditions, including Sufism, Christianity, and others. There is a Biblical reference to it in Jesus words in Romans. To me this may be a key to life, if not "the key." Right away, the I-ching hexagrams "The Traveler or Wanderer, and The Caldron" come to mind, but more on this later.

How do we journey through this life, living and functioning in this world, but not be of it? I think the meaning of it goes a lot deeper then people might realize. I don't pretend to know what the exact answers are, but maybe I can give some insight from my perspective. I mentioned the hexagram (56) of the I-ching called "The Traveler or Wanderer" and (50) "The Caldron." However the whole I-ching, and a lot of other holy books might be trying to point us to the way of achieving or returning to this state of not being "Of the world."

What is your world from a subjective point of view? I would put fourth the notion that the world as we see it is a reflection of everything that is inside us, as well as that of the collective consciousness surrounding us. When we are children or newborns, we are closer to, or are the pure essence, like a sparkling glass of clear water. As we become socially conditioned our pure essence becomes integrated with thoughts and projections of other entities. These range from our parents, to schools and religious institutions. As we progress through life everything is colored by these, lets call them introduced impurities. To put it simply, we forget who we are and become involved with the drama of life.

Our original essence, and connection to the ultimate essence is corrupted and made impure. We form what is called an ego, or false perception of who we are and what might really be important. Once this ego is formed, it seeks to propagate itself with things that please it, or make it feel comfortable. But do we really feel comfortable? Aren't we always searching to improve, keep our lot in life, or the status quot. As we approach the later years of life, questions can really start cropping up. Like for Instance; What's this all for? Where am I headed? When the quote: "world gets chaotic, and the people around us seem like strangers, we start asking the hard questions."

It's at this time that we realize that our involvement with "The world" may be an illusion. And that! my brothers, is exactly what it is. For the essence of your true self, is a light that has been covered a long time ago. How do we "return" to our true pure selves and uncover the light. Maybe this could be called re-enlightenment instead of enlightenment.

The I-Ching says we are wanderers or travelers, as in a foreign country. This hexagram called "Lu" in Chinese reminds us that we should be traveling through life like we are traveling through a foreign country. Strangers in a foreign land, are careful not to get sidetracked into difficult situations, or fall in with unsavory characters. The I-Ching hexagram "The Caldron" talks about sacrificing our ego and accepting guidance from a higher power.

Lets put this into a real time scenario. When we perceive anything in this so-called world, do we become emotionally involved, and let our senses instead of our "essence" rule us? Maybe the key is, living life from a detached or non-attached point of view. Everything we see before our eyes, and feel with our senses are in fact programmed illusions or perceptions. These are based on that belief system being formed since childhood.

So as we walk down the street, and see, say for instance, a homeless person. We might have several feelings come up, such as feelings of hurt, or feelings of fear. This would depend on our personal preconditioning. But what if we began to go through life as a wise traveler, looking at things like they are a motion picture? A projector projecting images on a screen. Are you doing the projecting, or maybe writing a script for phenomenon, and what is really just energy and a play of vibratory light? Because that's all "matter," or that homeless person is really. "The observer affects the observed." Not that you shouldn't have compassion, or be a non feeling person. But turn down the volume and live life "viewing" the world, and realize it for what it is every second your living it. The more you have awareness of the moment, and not just living in the moment, the quicker you will begin to perceive or

72

rediscover your own essence.

Its like a smelting process. We slowly remove the impurities of our preconditioning, by looking at each moment with a peaceful feeling of wonderment, and seeing the power of our own thoughts and what we can, or cannot do with them. Maybe another way to put it would be. What kind of sensory feelings are we projecting onto ourselves, and maybe others in each moment of whatever comes up in life. Be a simultaneous watcher of the world and your ego self, which essentially have become one in the same through preconditioning. Remember our essence is pure...some might call it our spirit. And our essence doesn't have anything to do with the world, which includes even our own body. Change the way you look at (view) things and the things you look at will change. And maybe you will discover your essence in the process.

Refuge in a troubled world

Sometimes inferior influences prevail in this surrounding phenomenon we call a world. Like what is described in the I-ching, hexagram number 12 "Pi" which is standstill. There are other hexagrams that are similar. Sometimes it's better to retreat into your higher self or to be still and meditate. We try to make things right when the flow isn't allowing us to. Why forge through the rapids, when sometimes it is better to guide your canoe over to the shore and take a rest. Let the storm blow over and the clouds clear. This gives us time to get out of the stream of chaotic energy surrounding us. It gives us time to center. It also gives us time to have an empty mind and relax. Get into the space of "not trying" by being what I call stress free, thought free, mind free, and body free, letting go, going on retreat. This doesn't mean you quit growing. In fact, this gives you time to grow while everything around you is standing still or worse yet, in chaos. Treat yourself nice, you deserve it. Don't let the imbalance in the world or around you take a toll. Let Great Spirit handle it. Sometimes we can be an inhabitant of the planet, but not of the world. If you get my meaning!

Natural Disasters, acts of God?

It's ironic that when there is a natural disaster, people say "Oh! that was an act of God." How so, I say? Do you mean that God sits up in the sky and commands nature to wreak havoc?
What's so funny is, that in the context of nature being one with the "Tao," "Great Spirit," or whatever is a comfortable name for you. It might well be called an act of God, in a natural sense. Not with thought out vengeance or purposeful harm, but as an act of the planet being herself.

Of course mother earth when confronted with pollution, wars, and general destruction of her resources, would react like any living organism, and proceed to correct things. How this is done, might be revealing itself. Of course there has always been natural occurrences. But when people get in the way, it becomes a disaster. Some things to consider are, over population, and what that population does to remain in harmony with the natural order of things. Balance inside may equal balance outside.

Native American's definition of Medicine

Although Native Americans accept the western view of the word medicine, their understanding is much broader and encompasses a context on which their tradition is based. This can include the presence and power embodied in, or demonstrated by a person, a place, an event, an object, or natural phenomenon. It can mean the power, potency, energy, or spirit of whatever event or object is being experienced. A common phrase being "that's good medicine." Seeing a hawk fly overhead while doing a ritual or prayer can be good medicine. Other things might fall into the "bad medicine" category. It really depends on the spirit involved. A medicine object can be beneficial to a healing process. Things such as a feather, a crystal, etc. The terms medicine man or woman can be confusing or ambiguous. Their are many kinds of healers. Some use herbs, while others may use words, or spiritual powers. I prefer the Lakota term "Wicasa Wakan" meaning holy or sacred man. This indicates someone who is a spiritual or a holy person, and pursues and serves the sacred and divine. The divine being great spirit, and all that is associated with the creator of all. Birds, flowers, herbs, and nature in general embodies the spirit of the creator. The term medicine man would more properly fit a grade B western movie. The healers in the Native American community are much more diverse and accomplished then some would believe. The western world of so called modern medicine is starting to come to terms with other healing modalities based in different cultures, but not fast enough.

The Integral Way

The definition of integral is: "consisting or composed of parts that together constitute a whole." When we start cultivating ourselves we integrate with the whole, and go beyond the duality. We look at the bigger picture and feel the oneness of all. This can be a healing process as we begin to go to the core level of our own being, integrating and accepting even our own feelings, and parts of ourselves. This is done with no judgment and brings about a feeling of wholeness within. It also helps in the process of cultivation, as things that we do battle with no longer have a hold. They dissolve in the oneness of the whole, and the negativity surrounding them disperses. When there is no opponent there is no battle. First we integrate then we cultivate which brings about a natural order and balance. Cultivation is acceptance, humility, and following our superior or higher self. Its all a process. Feel the oneness of self with nature, and the Tao.

Every Day is a lifetime

When we get up in the morning, we don't know how our day will progress, that is why it is good to have an adaptable attitude. How our day progresses may have to do with how we live it, that's why we should nurture the moment. It is said when we proceed to the next life we have no remembrance of the former. This is so we don't have too much on our mind or become overwhelmed in the life we are living. That's how we should live each day, putting away past memories, and concentrating on the moment. Inferior thoughts may arise sometimes and we should retreat from them until a time when it is more beneficial to move forward. A lot of times these thoughts arise when we are accomplishing something superior, or making progress along particular lines. Be aware of the moment, know when to proceed or retreat. Progress on matters important to you may seem slow sometimes. Make time work for you, when working on cultivating good habits. Sometimes its best to just bite off a little, other times you can take larger pieces. Regulation, moderation, cultivation are all good things. The less we become aroused by inferior thoughts the more balanced we will be, and life will be on more of an even footing for us. This brings a form of contentment and peace, no matter what is appearing in our life. Look at the duality. Be like water and fill up the deep spaces slowly so you can overcome them with time, and then flow on.

Pick Your Thoughts

What thoughts do you wish to be in your head or do you give power to? How about the thoughts you read? I have been reflecting a lot lately about what I write, and also about what I read. If you see or hear a thought that doesn't empower you, or make you feel good, just look at it and let it go. Those that do make you feel better, say to yourself yes I can be empowered with that, or that fits into my scheme of things. Thoughts are images so maybe you want to work with that particular image in your head. Never struggle with it, just let it happen, or let it go.

In my case I take myself way to seriously sometimes, as we all do from time to time. After all Great Spirit knows I'm not a saint, and if I was, it is said that in order to be a saint you have to have been a sinner. One of my friends has a blog and at the top he has sacred, profane, sacred, profane. I like the drift, two sides of a coin if you will. A little humor and sarcasm doesn't hurt either. So on that note I have decided to diversify a bit and start including more witty, humorous, and cynical stuff, in my life. This will include stuff by Mark Twain and many others. Life's to short. Yes I will still be beating the spiritual, ecological and ethnic drum as always, but hey it's all good. Not that anyone takes me that seriously anyway. And if at times you encounter a little profanity in life, remember, its one of two sides of the same coin. One thing you can be sure of, life and my writings will always be thought provoking.

"Ta Tay" the Wind

Ta'te (Ta TAY) the Wind, is the Messenger of Skan, Lakota God of the sky or the supreme authority. Sometimes ta'te is sent to stir things up and plant new seeds. Ta'te can also be associated with storms and thunder which have been discussed earlier in my writings. Ta'te is something that you can't see, but the effects are felt. Try standing on a bluff and let the wind clean your aura, by feeling it blowing through your body and carrying away all the stress and negativity. Ta'te is what is blown through the flute, and is expressed or manifested in a musical form to soothe the soul. The next time you feel the wind gently blowing across you face think of Great Spirit.

Of course the wind can be powerful as in a thunderstorm or tornado. That's why its so important to live in tune with nature, and (Maka) Mother earth.

What do you mean Spiritual?

How can you search for something you already are? If your
searching your not realizing that there is no way you can
Quote: "not be spiritual."... Yes You!! That's right with all
your thoughts and habits, both sacred and profane, naughty
and nice, good and evil, and on and on. Those are just
words. Don't accept a belief, and then beat yourself up, and
punish yourself because you didn't live up to it. Or reject
and hate others because they are different, or not on your
spiritual path. Get over it! Accept yourself for who you are.
You started out as a beautiful child, an empty clear glass,
and then all this "stuff" got poured into you, stirred around
and the glass became murky. After that it all settled to the
bottom, and every once in a while a piece floats to the
surface, and you go ouch, or you say, that's not me! It's all
you my friend, and there is no use in feeling guilty about all
that stuff, because deep down inside YOU ARE
SPIRITUAL! Love all parts of yourself and integrate it all,
so that it empowers you.

If you happen to find a part of yourself that feels guilt, fear,
and shame. Let your higher self, sage self, shaman self, or
whatever self you chose, intervene. Have a reasonable
conversation with this doubting part. Who knows you
better then you? A shrink, a guru, a minister? Not hardly!
Go within and have a good lively conversation, and you
will realize that you are the creator. Don't feel guilty about
being a spiritual being in the world's clothes? Feel good
and accept and love all parts of yourself. The Lakota have a
word for the ghost self (called "nagi") that wanders in
limbo until you accept it, nurture it, and give it a home. The
sooner you accept it, the happier you will be. You have
nothing to live up to except what others have planted in

your head. So yes they planted it there, and its part of you. And yes, its the little boy or girl feeling bad because they didn't live up to, or are trying to live up to, whatever. But the more you look at that "stuff" and the different aspects of your personality, you see more of the "clear water, and less of the murky stuff. Nothing is other then what you believe it to be, so just be yourself and love every bit of it. Feel good about who you are! Because in the final wash, you are that clear water in the Glass!

Pole Shift

What's going on with the planet, world, energy we are accustomed to? Why all the weird weather, earthquakes, tornadoes and just a feeling of unease on the planet. My friends feel it, do you? Imaginations gone wild? You decide. My theory is that with the latest discoveries of cracks in the polar ice cap, and the melting and breaking away of some large chunks of ice, something is changing on a deeper level then some would like to admit. Drought in a lot of areas too. This wasn't supposed to happen for decades by some accounts. Edgar Cayce, and the Hopi's mentioned this very thing happening around this time. The year 2012 has been mentioned, and I have been asked about it. Maybe the shifting of the poles would create a time warp too! I would think anything is possible, but I will leave that to the scientists. Maybe I shouldn't though, because their predictions and models about the ice cap and other things are way off. And I'm just talking about the natural things. And we are all connected to nature so it would affect all that is around us, including our moods, and maybe our energy. Is it scary? No, but it could wreak havoc, on a larger scale then what we already see. I guess we will all just have to be observers. Trying to correct this situation has been, and would be a challenge. Maybe the best thing to do now is just remain optimistic, because It might be for the best. I hope so, for the sake of my Grandchildren. Maybe it will usher in a change of consciousness and well being. Heck we might all get kicked into another dimension. Or maybe the original people that brought us here from the Pleiades, will come down and pick us up.

Natural Resources & Natural Disasters

Natural Resources
First I would like to touch on the Natural resources portion of this article. I heard that oil could go up so high that people that drive could end up paying 5 to 8 dollars a gallon at the pump. This will affect other modes of transportation like trucks and trains. People are suffering folks, and guess what? All this shortage of the natural resources of oil, if in fact there is a shortage, is going to have an effect on every man, women, and child in this country.

Higher prices will prevail in all areas that are on the tail end of this irresponsible occurrence. High food prices occur because again the trucks and trains that deliver our food won't be able to. The cost of refrigeration is going up. The cost of anything made of petroleum products is going up. That would include all plastics, plastic containers, etc. which most of our food is packaged in.

This is not a time for the fainthearted. Its is a time for people to wake up. Now I know I have been talking a lot about peaceful revolutions, and Gandhi type protests and sending love. And all these things are still good, but now I am going to change the dynamic a little and partake in the duality. This is just unconscionable and totally uncalled for. As is the situation with the disaster in Burma or Myanmar which I will get to later.

This is about survival of the poor, the elderly, those on fixed incomes, and the general population. When you look at the cost of man's inhumanity to man by the different means that have arisen, people need to do more then just speak out. They need to take matters into their own hands. War and mismanagement, along with greed, seems to be the cause of the critical situation facing us all. The effect from the phony war on terrorism in Iraq and the residual aftermath, might just create chaos in America and in the world at large. I suggest families contact one another and get ready or prepare themselves for the worst. Am I buying into fear tactics being propagated by the powers to be? To quote an ancient oracle "When the wicked are in control the people will suffer"

Natural disasters
The situation in Myanmar puts a lot of things in perspective. Now they are saying that there are a million homeless, and over 100,000 dead, with a greedy military in control that kept aid from getting in and helping those poor souls. Think about that a minute, ONE MILLION people homeless. How many more will die? If there ever was a need for a just war, it would be to go in and clean house on the people holding up the progress of aid and red cross efforts. Yes this was a natural disaster, but its how you handle these things that counts. Then there are the tornadoes in the U.S. that have killed 97 already, a record high for this time of year.

Would you say that the planet seems a little unbalanced right now? Is it a reflection of the unbalanced consciousness of the people on Mother earth?
I will leave that for he reader to decide. I hope there is someone out there reading this and passing it on, because that might be the only way my thoughts get to the public. Its is up to each person on this planet to spread the word, so we can form a consensus and consider possible solutions. I have been getting a lot of feed back on my writing, and I

will continue to do it because I care.

God Religion & Enlightenment

Ok folks this could be a long one, but I will try to distill it. There has been a shift going on what I have perceived lately regarding Jesus, who's real name is Yeshua, or Yehoshua. Or maybe a shift in the whole spiritual view of religions, Christianity and God. My take on it has been one that has grown over the years, but as of late has acquired new dimensions through self realization, meditation and a whole lot of reading. Instead of making statements, I will ask questions and make statements you can ponder. Lets start with Yeshua. He was a rebel, an apostate, he spoke from the heart, and he was a man of peace. He was hated by the religious establishment of his day, and his own fellow Jews. Let me put a caveat on that, the pious Jewish leaders who didn't listen, and turned others against him. Let him who has ears listen and hear. The words he spoke were ones of direction, explanation, and mystery's that might not have been meant to be understood until this time period. He even said when asked by the disciples what things meant, that it would be a mystery to a lot of people.

Since the finding of the dead sea scrolls and the Nag Hammadi discoveries, books have been unearthed that lend a different slant to things. One that comes to mind is the Gospel of Thomas. These are just the condensed sayings of Christ or yeshua without any religious dogma added. In other words, no dying on the cross for our sins, no explanation of anything that is associated with the dogma of today's christian movement. No condemnation, guilt, control, or manipulative attempts. Now when you look at a distilled version of what he had to say in Thomas, along with other sources Like the Aramaic words he spoke, and of the different, colorful, and beautiful meanings those have. You start to get a different picture. You start to get this picture of an enlightened master, who was trying to show us things.

This brings up the question of was he God's literal son? Was he divine? Was he an enlightened soul who had a purpose to fulfill. The gospels that we have in our bibles today were, manipulated into the Bible by Emperor Constantine around 325 A.D. at the council of Nicea. Evidently Constantine wanted to reshape the movement that was born out of Christ for his own selfish purposes. Off of that sprung the church of Rome along with all the Hierarchical trappings and control of the people. It was all about control. The stuff that went on during this time is too extensive to go into, and there are much better books on this subject then I could write here. But the bottom line is, a lot of the books that could have been included in the Bible were discarded. Some of them from the Gnostic (Gnosis meaning Knowledge or hidden Knowledge) movement, which saw a much deeper meaning then what was written in the books Constantine included.

These books sometimes referred to things that Jesus implied. Ideas like the kingdom of heaven being within us. Constantine couldn't use those books because if the kingdom was within, and God was within, like Jesus said Quote: "I and the father are one." Then what would Constantine use to control the people, because he wanted everything to be external. Obey the commandments or burn in hell. Accept Christ as Savior or burn in hell. Do what the church says. Feel guilt and fear, or God will punish you, and a whole host of things. Some of the gospels chosen could have even been manipulated to include dogma, and may not have been written by Mathew or John or whoever.

Most of then were written decades after Christ was gone.

So with all that being said, and check my facts, don't take my word for it. Was Yeshua here for a different reason then we think. Was he here to point the way to what I call Transformation, Transcendence, and Truth. Think of the cross as a "T" and think of the three crosses on the hill as three "T's" Transcendence, Transformation and Truth. That came to me in a vision.

Now when you think about it, Christianity or a lot of churches and Christians don't represent these ideals, and the ideals of the sayings of Christ and the actions of Christ. He said love thy neighbor, but they say lets go to war and kill, he said love thy enemies, but they say God's on our side. He said The kingdom of heaven is not over here or over there but something you can't see, and that the Kingdom of heaven is within you. And they say you won't make it to the kingdom if you don't do this or do that, and you will go to hell, or be destroyed! Christ said God was loving and merciful. They say God is angry, punishing, and sometimes even condones evil acts. Who would you rather believe? Is there any question?

Now you might say, why is Thunderhands talking about christian things and not Native American beliefs? Well, you might be surprised to learn what some of the native beliefs are. They have many of the same concepts of another system that doesn't judge, and that is Taoism, an eastern viewpoint. And when you look at some of the enlightening things the Native American says or believes, and the Taoist's philosophy, you find a close resemblance. And that is Nature with a capitol "N." You find sayings that are incredible and loving. One that comes to mind and I am paraphrasing some of this. "You whites tend to believe that when man was created Great Spirit breathed into him the breath of life, but we believe his breath took in all of nature as well." Well Isn't that profound. The "Tao" often time associates things with the elements of wood, wind, water, fire, etc. The Tao te Ching speaks of water and nature, and other natural elements, like thunder, and lightening. It's funny Jesus called James & John "The sons of thunder." Jesus often spoke of crops, and the wheat and fire. And he picked fisherman as some of his disciples. He walked on water, and there were storms and lightening and thunder from the heavens. Open your eyes, Jesus' sayings were steeped in nature.

Thunder is big in native American culture, it represents a shock sometimes, or waking up, or a cleansing and a calm after the storm. And so it is with the I-Ching. Thunder beings are powerful beings featured on totem poles in the form of Thunderbirds. Drums are used in ceremony, as ritualistic thunderous drums. The Lakota say that the first great mystery of the 16 great mysteries is the Sun, and everything was created from then on. Sometimes that sun is looked at as son or s-o-n, or Tunkashila. Many of the beliefs seem eastern, and so many believe that the Native American came from the east over the land bridge that once existed up by the Aleutian Island chain. And wasn't Yeshua eastern or from the east. And where did he travel, and what did he pick up during all those years that are missing in the Bible. Its funny they are missing isn't it? You would think that the Bible writers would have included that. I mean those are the informative years. It doesn't make sense does it? It's like someone wanted to cut that part of the picture out. But you never know what's going to be found on the splicing room floor.

So does religion today espouse the real teachings of Christ or are they in the same bag of trying to strike fear, condemnation, guilt and control. Or maybe they want a lot of money when they pass the plate. Do they support the powers to be, and war and hate. And do they stand Idly by and watch the planet destroyed by greed, corruption and war. And at times through history did they kill thousands in the name of Christ during the crusades. And how about the inquisition, and burning people at the stake. What do you think Yeshua would say or think about that? Get behind me Satan! Why does the church profile and hate certain groups of people as not worthy. Jesus hung out with prostitutes and tax collectors and those considered low life.

Now I know there are a lot of sincere people that are Christians, and I am not here to judge anyone, or any system, because it's all an illusion anyway. But if you were to call anything the anti-Christ. It wouldn't be a person it would be those who represented themselves as speaking for Christ, but then did just the opposite.

It's not about religion, it's about enlightenment. It's about love and all those who speak of love. It's about living in accordance with nature within yourself, and without. Its not about four walls with a roof and steeple. It's about Grandmother earth and Grandfather sky and all of creation. Jesus spoke of wolves in sheep's clothing. He warned against being mislead. Broad is the road to destruction narrow the road to life. The Indians have a name for the good Road, it is called the "Red Road." Look what's being done to the planet today and to the people on it. Where is the love?

So the shift I am seeing that I mentioned at the beginning is a shift in consciousness about Christ or Jesus and religion. And I see a lot of people waking up. And a lot of people are writing books now about the lessons we can learn from Jesus words and how to really understand what he was saying, and about how religion is a middleman that isn't needed. But if the consciousness shifts and people start connecting and loving one another, think of the possibilities. The government is sadly inadequate in spiritual matters. They are part of the problem, not the solution. They speak with a forked tongue. Just like they did when they committed genocide on the original inhabitants of America. When the shift is complete they will either sink or swim. The politicians speak of God and Jesus out of one side of their mouth, and declare war out of the other. What have they really done for the homeless? Jesus spoke of the good Samaritan. What about the elderly on fixed incomes? Need I go further, and that's just scratching the surface. Do you want to live in the kingdom that Yeshua spoke of. Then disavow all that you see around you. Be non-attached and go within. Ignore the duality so that you can change yourself inside and see that change take affect outside. As above so below. Be a Christ, by using you Christ consciousness. Cast away all the negativity that you see around you in the media, the government, the schools and religion. Be reborn not born again. Pretty shocking isn't it. But remember my name is thunderhands, thunder shocks and hands create, by writing, and by other means like my drums. So maybe I'm beating a different kind of drum. Drums were used for communication you know? Somebody has to speak from the heart, which also beats like a drum.

Speaking from the Heart

Invariably something arises every day that gives me pause to reflect on a certain situation, about myself and others. I practice what I call speaking from the heart. Sometimes it's with friends, other times with family. I get into trouble by doing this at times, unless the party I am talking to really understands what I am trying to say. With family you have to be careful it seems, that things aren't taken the wrong way. I guess with anybody for that matter. I won't go into personal details, but when you speak from the heart you have a tendency not to hold things back. Sometimes people take what you say to their heart and everything is OK. If what you say hurts someone, or strikes a chord they don't like, it can cause separation for a period of time. In certain cases what you are saying may be to purge what is perceived by one's self as trauma or feelings that need to be vented in the spirit of healing. I always try to preface comments with a thought that indicates that I am speaking for the good of everyone involved. If done correctly a healing can take place on certain levels. Its a touchy thing, because often what you mean to say can be diluted or distorted by the fact that words don't always convey the meaning you intended. Its like that saying "words are but crumbs from the feast of the mind." I have had situations where when talking with family, things are perceived as coming from a place of ego or manipulation, when in fact that wasn't the case at all. Its hard to tell how people will take things because we are all so different, and we all have that ego that has its own agenda. At times I have had my own immediate family disown or distance themselves from me and the things I intended to convey. With my siblings it could be a perception formed from childhood, that one person was favored over another by the parents that raised us, when in fact that might not be true. Social conditioning and parenting play a big part in our lives. Ego's feel threatened, particularly regarding matters of shall I say spirit or spirituality. I think the key to understanding one another is to take it in the spirit it was meant. I always leave the door open for discussion after a conversation with friends and family. Because no matter how good our intention, we might not have conveyed it in a fashion that doesn't "tread on the tail of the tiger" (I-Ching). I would like to think that dialog will somehow overcome any misunderstandings. Also I have found that everything will be fine until a third party gets involved that has no idea of the relationship that you have established between the person you intended to communicate certain things to, and yourself. Its all a growth process. One of the greatest and wisest men of all time, Jesus or Yeshua was misunderstood by many to the point of his death. Sometimes he said or did things that he felt needed to be conveyed for a healing to take place. I like the spirit of the saying, never let the sun set until that feeling of anger or misunderstanding can be dispersed. We are all here for a certain period of time. We don't know from one day to the next how long that will be. But certainly we wouldn't want a division or hard feelings to exist for to long because of this very simple fact. Impermanence is part of life so lets try to be at peace with all of our brothers and sisters on the planet. This includes everyone and not just immediate family. And when I use the term immediate, I mean related by blood. However even that term can cause division, because we are all family. We are all one, connected by Great Spirit or the Tao. Maybe the reason misunderstandings occur is that this fact isn't realized. We are a mirror of ourselves. So when someone speaks to us and it strikes a chord, maybe we shouldn't make it good or bad. Its just a learning process.

94

Like I said earlier we can bypass the duality and look at the big picture. Acceptance, understanding, love, and at the same time detachment. Great Spirit often uses us in ways that can't always be comprehended at the time. So reflect or contemplate on what others may be conveying, because its like we are talking to ourselves. Its the spirit of the law not the law. Nobody is more holy then the other, but we can give credit where credit is due. And that's to the higher power or the Tao, for guiding us in whatever way it uses to manifest the lessons we or others learn in life. Don't just see what you want to see through the eyes of your conditioning, look beyond that and find the pearls of wisdom being conveyed through that source.

Buddha & Christ Mind

When you say a prayer or make supplication to the deity, there are certain things you should remember. Remember that your essence or spirit is actually the Christ or Buddha within. That's why in Zen they say Buddha mind or Christ mind if you will, because that very same spirit is within you or is you. Through years of conditioning we forget who we are. We become accustomed to thinking that our ego is us, when in reality our "essence" is the true self or the true mind. That's why when some bow to the Buddha or make supplication to Christ it is really what that image represents that we are paying homage to. That image represents what our true capability is. Its a reminder to us. Meditation or just being still is the only approach that allows us to see the thoughts and habits that get in the way of that clear being or essence within. To catch a glimpse is to be inspired. Little glimpses over time allow us to see longer ones. This is the way to walk the path and allow that essence or light to come through. Be as a child again, have the innocence of a child, and you will regain your true heritage which is Buddha mind or Christ mind.

Additional Information and products

Music CD's & Books By Thunderhands
Books

"Listen to the Wind Speak from the Heart"
Order from: www.wakiyarecords.com
www.spiritofcrazyhorse.com

CD's
Desert Spirits-Native American Flute & percussion
Tribal Unity-Native American Flute & Percussion
Available at Amazon as mp3 Downloads
Or at
www.wakiyarecords.com

Websites
www.spiritofcrazyhorse.com
www.thenativeamericanTaoist.com
http://apachetracker.blogspot.com/

Contact Thunderhands for Info or Bookings.
thunderhands@thenativeamericantaoist.com

Notes:

Notes

Notes

5144152R0

Made in the USA
Lexington, KY
08 April 2010